THE LIBRARY OF
WOLVES AND WILD DOGS ™

THE ARCTIC WOLF

Fred H. Harrington

The Rosen Publishing Group's
PowerKids Press ™
New York

To Dave Mech, who first introduced me to gray wolves in northern Minnesota when he took me on as a graduate student several decades ago, and who recently invited me to join him on a quest for arctic wolves on Ellesmere Island. No one knows the Arctic wolf as well as Dave.

Published in 2002 by The Rosen Publishing Group, Inc.
29 East 21st Street, New York, NY 10010

First Edition

Project Editor: Emily Raabe
Book Design: Michael de Guzman

Photo Credits: p. 4 © Alan & Sandy Carey/Peter Arnold Inc.; p. 7 © S.J. Krasemann/Peter Arnold Inc.; pp. 8, 11, 12 © L. David Mech; pp. 14, 15, 20 © Staffan Widstrand/CORBIS; p. 16 © Brian Vickander/CORBIS; p. 19 © Joe McDonald/CORBIS; pp. 19 (Peary caribou), 19 (Arctic wolf), 19 (timber wolf) © Animals Animals; p. 22 © Erwin & Peggy Bauer.

Harrington, Fred H.
  The arctic wolf / Fred H. Harrington.—1st ed.
    p. cm. — (The library of wolves and wild dogs)
  ISBN 0-8239-5766-7 (lib. bdg.)
  1. Wolves—Arctic regions—Juvenile literature. [1. Wolves. 2. Zoology—Arctic regions.] I. Title. II Series.
  QL737.C22 H366 2002
  599.773'0911'3—dc21
                                                                        00-012334

Manufactured in the United States of America

Contents

What Are Arctic Wolves?

There are three **species**, or kinds, of wolves. These three species are gray wolves, red wolves, and Ethiopian wolves. Arctic wolves are a type of gray wolf that lives in the far north. They sometimes are called a **subspecies** of gray wolf. This means that they are alike in many ways. For example, all gray wolves, including Arctic wolves, live in families called packs. Each pack lives in its own area, called a **territory**. All gray wolves also hunt **prey** animals that are larger than they are, such as deer and **caribou**. Gray wolves all can **mate** with one another and have puppies. Arctic wolves are different from other gray wolves, however. For one thing, their coats are white. They have **adapted** to their **habitat** on the **Arctic tundra**.

All Arctic wolves have white coats. This adaptation helps them to blend in with the snow on the Arctic tundra.

The Arctic Tundra

The Arctic can be very cold and dark. During winter, the sun doesn't shine and the ground is frozen solid. In summer, the sun shines 24 hours each day. It gets warmer, but only the top foot or two (half meter) of the ground thaws. Many animals only visit the Arctic during the summer, when it's sunny and warm. Some, though, live there all year. Arctic wolves live there year-round. They have adapted to the cold and darkness of the Arctic. They have dense, white fur, even between their toes, to keep them warm. They have short, rounded ears and shorter **muzzles** and legs than other gray wolves, so they lose less heat. They even have special layers of **cells** in their eyes that help them see by moonlight or by the **northern lights** during the dark winter.

You can see for miles (km) on the Arctic tundra because there are no trees. Only short grasses, flowers, berries, and willows grow there.

Life on the Edge

Arctic wolves live in packs, like other wolves and wild dogs. A pack is a family, with a mother and father wolf and their puppies. Raising a family in the Arctic is not easy. In warmer habitats outside the Arctic, a gray wolf mother usually gives birth every year. She usually has a **litter** of five or six puppies in late April or early May. In the Arctic, a mother Arctic wolf has only two or three puppies in late May or early June, when spring finally comes. In some years she might not have puppies at all! She only has puppies if she had enough food to eat during the winter. When her puppies grow up, they stay with the pack for several years. They help their parents care for the next litter of puppies, who are their younger brothers and sisters.

 Arctic wolf puppies are born with a brownish coat and blue eyes. As adults, their eyes turn golden brown and their coats turn white.

Frozen Ground and Rocky Dens

All gray wolves have their puppies in dens. Timber wolves can dig their dens deep in the ground. Arctic wolves can't dig their dens in the ground because the ground is always frozen solid just below the surface. This forces Arctic wolves to make the most of their dens in rock caves. Rock caves aren't easy to find, so Arctic wolves may use some caves over and over again. Scientists found bones in one rock cave on Ellesmere Island in Canada that probably were left there by wolves at least 800 years ago! When wolves don't have a rock den to use, they might dig just a shallow pit in which the puppies can stay. Pit dens don't have a roof to protect the puppies from bad weather, but they do have steep sides to keep the puppies from crawling away.

Arctic wolf puppies, like these puppies shown here, usually are born in rock caves that are above ground.

Feeding the Puppies

Arctic wolves are **predators**. This means they kill other animals for food. Arctic hares, Peary caribou, and musk oxen are their favorite prey. Arctic wolves must travel many miles (km) each day to find their prey. The territory that an Arctic wolf pack searches is huge. For you, having a territory as big as an Arctic wolf's would mean having a backyard 20 miles (32 km) long on each side! When adult wolves bring back food to the puppies, they carry the food in their stomachs so they can trot along at 6 miles (10 km) per hour without dropping any food. Puppies rush out of the den and lick the adults around the muzzle. This makes the adults **regurgitate**, or cough up, the food to the hungry puppies.

Arctic wolf puppies are able to eat regurgitated meat when they are about one month old.

Catch Me If You Can

Arctic hares are one of the Arctic wolves' prey animals. They are very large rabbits. They can weigh as much as 12 pounds (5.4 kg). They have white fur year-round. White fur helps the hares blend into the snow in winter, but in summer, wolves can see Arctic hares from miles (km) away. Arctic hares can see the white wolves, too. The hares stand up and hop on their hind legs, so they can watch for wolves. This makes them hard to catch. Arctic hare babies are called leverets. Arctic wolves like to hunt leverets because they are easier to catch. Leverets are gray when they are little, so they blend in with the colors of rocks. Arctic hare mothers hide their leverets among rocks so wolves don't find all of them. When they are bigger and faster, leverets turn white. Arctic hares travel in groups, sometimes with 100 hares in a single group. With many eyes watching for danger, hares are a lot safer from hungry Arctic wolves.

Some animals in the Arctic, such as the Arctic fox, turn brown in the summer to blend in when the snow is gone. Arctic hares and Arctic wolves both stay white all year.

Shaggy Beasts

Musk oxen have long, shaggy fur, big heads, and sharp, pointed horns. Adults can weigh up to 800 pounds (363 kg). A big Arctic wolf weighs only about 100 pounds (45 kg), so catching a healthy, adult musk ox is difficult. Musk ox calves are much smaller. They are easier for wolves to catch, but adult musk oxen have a very special way to protect them. When wolves attack, the adult musk

oxen form a circle with their calves in the middle. They lower their heads so their sharp horns point out, making it hard for the wolves to catch a calf. If the musk oxen stand their ground, the wolves search for another group. If the musk oxen panic and run, the wolves might be able to catch a calf or even an adult. When that happens, the wolves have plenty of food to eat.

 Musk oxen are the biggest prey animals for Arctic wolves.

Miniature 'Reindeer'

Animals that live in the Arctic are often smaller than related animals that live farther south. Arctic wolves, for example, are smaller than other gray wolves that live south of the Arctic. The same is true for caribou, which are cousins of reindeer. Peary caribou, prey of the gray wolves, live in the Arctic. They are very small. Arctic animals are smaller because they can't find as much food as animals that live in milder climates. Peary caribou eat willows and lichen. These plants grow slowly in the Arctic. Snow covers them in the winter so the caribou have to dig up snow to find food. This can be exhausting. Peary caribou live in small groups so they can keep watch while they dig for food. They run if they see wolves approaching.

The barren-ground caribou (top left) *is much larger than the Peary caribou* (top right) *that lives in the Arctic. The Arctic wolf* (bottom left) *is smaller than the gray timber wolf* (bottom right).

When Times Are Tough

Cold temperatures, short summers, and long, dark winters make the Arctic a harsh place to live. Arctic animals are adapted for those harsh conditions. During winter, hares, caribou, and musk oxen dig through snow to find their food. In most years, they can find enough food to survive the winter. In some years, however, ice storms in early winter cover the animals' food with a thick layer of ice. When this happens, the prey animals can't eat. Many of them starve before spring comes. In other years, winter comes too early and snow covers the plants. This also will cause many young hares, musk ox calves, and caribou calves to die. If the prey animals die, the wolves are left without food. Without enough prey to eat, wolves are too hungry to have puppies in the spring.

This hungry Arctic wolf will have to spend much of its time searching for food in the frozen Arctic.

The Future

Arctic wolves have survived for thousands of years. They have adapted to the harsh climate of their home. There is one thing that might threaten the survival of the Arctic wolves, however. This threat is **climate** change. The world is getting warmer. This is partly because people are burning a lot of oil to heat their houses and lots of gasoline to run their cars. Burning these fuels causes what is called **global warming**. Scientists believe that global warming will cause more ice storms in the Arctic. If that happens, prey animals will suffer. In 1961, scientists believed there were more than 24,000 Peary caribou in the Arctic. Today they think there are fewer than 2,000. These scientists believe a bad ice storm in 1995 killed many caribou and musk oxen. If we have too many bad storms, all the Arctic animals, including wolves, may be in trouble.

Glossary

adapted (uh-DAP-ted) Changed to fit new conditions.

Arctic tundra (ARK-tik TUN-druh) Land with grasses, low-growing plants, and no trees near the northern edge of North America, Europe, and Asia.

caribou (KAHR-uh-boo) A type of deer that lives in the north. Both males and females have antlers.

cells (SELZ) One of many tiny units that make up all living things.

climate (KLY-mit) The kind of weather a certain area has.

global warming (GLOH-buhl WAR-ming) A gradual increase in the average temperature of Earth. It is caused by gases that are released when people burn fuels such as gasoline.

habitat (HA-bih-tat) The surroundings where an animal or plant naturally lives.

litter (LIH-tur) A group of baby animals born to the same mother at the same time.

mate (MAYT) When a male and female join together to make babies.

muzzles (MUH-zuhlz) The part of animals' heads that extends forward and contains the nose.

northern lights (NOR-thern LYTS) White, green, and red bands of light that sometimes occur in the night sky in northern regions of the world.

predators (PREH-duh-terz) Animals that kill other animals for food.

prey (PRAY) Animals that are hunted by other animals for food.

regurgitate (re-GUR-juh-tayt) To vomit, or throw up, partly eaten food.

species (SPEE-sheez) A single kind of plant or animal. For example, all people are one species.

subspecies (SUB-spee-sheez) A group of animals that are similar but have some differences.

territory (TEHR-uh-tohr-ee) Land or space protected by an animal for its use.

Index

Web Sites

To learn more about Arctic wolves, check out these Web sites:
www.enchantedlearning.com/subjects/mammals/dog/Arcticwolfprintout.shtml
www.goals.com/thayer/wolves/wolvesfm.htm
www.wolf.org